THE OFFICIAL
WEST HAM UNITED
ANNUAL 2016

Written by Rob Pritchard
Designed by Jon Dalrymple

A Grange Publication

© 2015. Published by Grange Communications Ltd., Edinburgh, under licence from West Ham United Football Club. Printed in the EU.

Photographs © West Ham United Football Club, Getty Images and Action Images.

ISBN 978-1-910199-57-2

Contents

WEST HAM UNITED OFFICIAL ANNUAL 2016

THIS ANNUAL BELONGS TO:

....

MY AGE:

....

MY SCHOOL:

....

MY FOOTBALL TEAM:

....

MY POSITION:

....

MY FAVOURITE WEST HAM UNITED PLAYER:

....

WHERE WEST HAM UNITED WILL FINISH IN THE BARCLAYS PREMIER LEAGUE:

....

Slaven Bilic

The West Ham United manager is delighted and proud to be back at a special, family Club

I am very proud to be the manager of West Ham United.

West Ham is a special Club. Wherever I have gone, I have always said that some of the best days of my football life were during my time with West Ham as a player.

I was here for 18 months and the bond I feel with this Club is like one I have felt with only two others in my career and that is my hometown club Hajduk Split and in the two years I had with Besiktas in Turkey.

The bond I feel with West Ham is personal, it is emotional. I felt it when I played here and I have felt it again every day since I was appointed as manager.

I felt that bond get even stronger when I was introduced to you at the Boleyn Ground in the summer. The welcome you gave me was special and I hope to repay that welcome with goals, wins and entertaining football.

This is a family Club and I am sure many of you reading this Annual support West Ham because other members of your family have done so – grandparents, parents, uncles, aunts, brothers and sisters.

The reason so many people follow this Club is because West Ham has embraced the ways of modern football, but at the same time it has not forgotten what makes us love football in the first place – the passion, the honour, the entertainment.

Every day I have spent with West Ham is a special experience. When I played in the famous Claret and Blue, the fans not only wanted us to win, but win with style. Now, as the manager, I want my West Ham team to do the same – to play good football and to win matches.

Thank you again for welcoming me back to West Ham United.

Slaven Bilic
Manager

Summer Signings

Get to know the players who joined West Ham United in the summer of 2015

West Ham United tooled up for the final season at the Boleyn Ground by bringing in an impressive group of summer signings.

France midfielder Dimitri Payet, young Spanish midfield player Pedro Obiang, Ireland goalkeeper Darren Randolph, Scotland U21 left-back Stephen Hendrie and Norway U18 attacker Martin Samuelsen all arrived in east London to bolster Slaven Bilic's squad.

Here, you can find out more about the newest Hammers with our fast facts...

Dimitri Payet

- Born on the island of Reunion situated in the Indian Ocean.
- Has spent almost his entire professional career in French football.
- Voted into the Ligue 1 Team of the Year in 2012/13 and 2014/15.

- His birthplace is Alcalá de Henares in central Spain.
- Was with Spanish giants Atletico Madrid then moved to Italian club Sampdoria at age 16.
- Has represented Spain at U17, U19 and U21 levels.

Pedro Obiang

Darren Randolph

- Born in the seaside town of Bray, County Wicklow, Republic of Ireland.
- Went to Presentation College in Bray.
- Represented Republic of Ireland at U15, U16, U17, U18, U19, U21, B and senior levels!

- Totalled 117 first-team appearances for his first professional club Hamilton Academical.
- Senior debut for Hamilton at age 16 and 7 months in a 2-0 Scottish Challenge Cup win over Queen's Park at Hampden Park in July 2011.
- Has been capped by Scotland at U17, U19 and U21 levels.

Stephen Hendrie

- Born in April 1997 in the town of Haugesund on Norway's west coast.
- Began his career with hometown club SK Vard as a schoolboy.
- Spent three seasons with Manchester City prior to joining West Ham United.
- Has represented his native Norway at U16, U17 and U18 levels.

Martin Samuelsen

- Hails from Ituzaingo in Buenos Aires, Argentina.
- Came through the ranks at River Plate - the club which produced the likes of Javier Mascherano and Alfredo Di Stefano.
- Nicknamed 'The Jewel' for his dazzling quick feet.

Manuel Lanzini

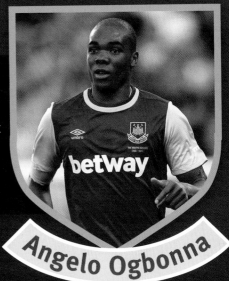

- Born in the central Italian city of Cassino in May 1988.
- Started off with Torino, where he made 147 league appearances and helped the club win promotion to Serie A.
- Moved across Turin to play for Juventus, where he was part of the squad which made last season's UEFA Champions League final.
- Capped ten times by Italy and took a runners-up medal from Euro 2012.

Angelo Ogbonna

Hammer of the Year

Aaron Cresswell completed a memorable treble at the 2014/15 West Ham United Player Awards

Few players have made as big and as instant an impact on the Barclays Premier League in recent seasons as Aaron Cresswell.

West Ham United's left-back enjoyed an outstanding debut top-flight campaign in 2014/15 following his arrival from Championship club Ipswich Town.

The Liverpool-born player completed all 38 of the Hammers' Barclays Premier League fixtures, catching the eye of teammates, opponents, pundits and supporters alike with his strong defending, relentless running and technical ability.

In a season during which Diafra Sakho, Cheikhou Kouyaté and Adrian, among others, also shone consistently, it was Cresswell who has shone more consistently than them all.

FACTFIL

Name: AARON CRESSWELL

Born: 15 December 1989, Liverpool, England

Clubs: Tranmere Rovers (80 apps, 6 goals), Ipswich Town (138 apps, 7 goals), West Ham United (42 apps, 2 goals

Individual honours:

Ipswich Town Player of the Year (2011/12), Championship Team of the Season (2013/14), Hammer of the Year, Players' Player of the Year, Signing of the Season (2014/1

*Stats correct to end of 2014/15 seasor

@Aaron_Cresswe

#HOTY201

10

As such, it was fitting that the No3 should end his debut season in England's top division by completing a dazzling Player Awards hat-trick by winning Hammer of the Year, sponsored by Betway, Players' Player of the Year, sponsored by AsMatt Limited, and Signing of the Season, sponsored by S14 VIP.

Speaking to West Ham TV after being crowned Hammer of the Year at the London Hilton on Park Lane, the defender summed up his maiden Claret and Blue campaign.

"As a season, it could not have gone any better for me," he confirmed. "To pick three awards up at a Club like West Ham is massive – not only to pick up Players' Player, which is one of the best awards you can get because you play with the players and train with them every day, but to top it off I won Hammer of the Year.

"It's a massive achievement for me. There are some fantastic players in our squad, so to get three awards is a real privilege.

"Making my Premier League debut was up there and something I had dreamt of since I was a little boy. That was the proudest moment of my career so far."

Being named Players' Player of the Year in his first season at the Club also illustrated just how highly and widely respected Cresswell is in the West Ham dressing room.

Quietly-spoken, determined and seldom injured, the left-back is a true professional.

"As I said during my speech at the Player Awards, from the first minute I walked in the lads have been great with me and welcomed me with open arms.

"I said to myself 'Keep your head down and work hard' and hopefully that's all paid off. To get three awards is massive."

*You can watch all the best bits from the 2014/15 Player Awards on West Ham TV, for FREE.

Roll of Honour

Goal of the Season

ENNER VALENCIA

Sponsored by England Environmental Services

Young Hammer of the Year

REECE BURKE

Sponsored by Ark Build PLC

Top Goalscorer

DIAFRA SAKHO

Sponsored by Mulalley

Best Team Performance

V MANCHESTER CITY (H), BARCLAYS PREMIER LEAGUE, 25 OCTOBER 2014

Sponsored by Shore Capital

Signing of the Season

AARON CRESSWELL

Sponsored by S14 VIP

Dylan Tombides Award

REECE OXFORD

Save of the Season

ADRIÁN

v

Chelsea (A), Barclays Premier League, 26 December 2014

Sponsored by Higgins

Best Individual Performance

CHEIKHOU KOUYATE

v

Manchester United (H), Barclays Premier League, 8 February 2015

Sponsored by Peter Rayney Tax Consulting

Players' Player of the Year

AARON CRESSWELL

Sponsored by AsMatt Ltd

Lifetime Achievement Award

MARTIN PETERS MBE

Sponsored by ACL

Hammer of the Year
AARON CRESSWELL

Sponsored by Betway

Aaron Cresswell was not the only winner at West Ham United's 2015 Player Awards, brought to you by Betway, in aid of the Academy.

Cresswell took home the Hammer of the Year, Players' Player of the Year and Signing of the Season trophies, beating off the challenge of runner-up Adrian and third-placed Enner Valencia for the fans' vote for their player of the season.

Elsewhere, on a night that saw tens of thousands of pounds raised for the Academy of Football, one of its finest-ever graduates Martin Peters MBE was presented with the third annual Lifetime Achievement Award **(1)**.

Peters, who was born in Plaistow and joined the Club as a schoolboy in the 1950s, made 364 West Ham appearances, scored exactly 100 goals and won both the 1965 European Cup Winners' Cup and 1966 FIFA World Cup.

Save of the Season maker Adrian **(2)** caught another well-deserved trophy, while Cheikhou Kouyate won Best Individual Performance for his display against Manchester United **(3)**, while Enner Valencia's rocket-shot at Hull City won him Goal of the Season **(4)**.

The Best Team Performance award was presented to goalscorers Morgan Amalfitano and Diafra Sakho for the 2-1 home win over Manchester City **(5 & 6)**.

Reece Burke completed a memorable season by being named Young Hammer of the Year **(7)**, while Reece Oxford scooped the Dylan Tombides Award for the outstanding Academy player of the season **(8)**.

*For exclusive interviews, features and behind the scenes video and photos from the 2014/15 Player Awards, use the hashtag #HOTY2015 on our official Twitter, Facebook and Instagram accounts.

West Ham United...

...How It Was Formed

West Ham United as we know it was officially formed in the summer of 1900

For its first five years, the Club we now know as West Ham United was known as Thames Ironworks FC – the works football team of the Thames Ironworks and Shipbuilding Company Limited.

Founded by the company's owner Arnold Hills and foreman Dave Taylor, Thames Ironworks competed in local leagues for five years, playing at three different stadia in east London.

In June 1900 the original football club was wound-up. The following month, West Ham United was incorporated as a company on 5 July 1900 and began a 15-year association with the Southern League at the dawn of the Edwardian era.

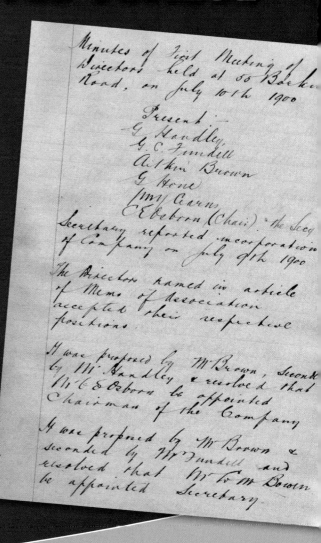

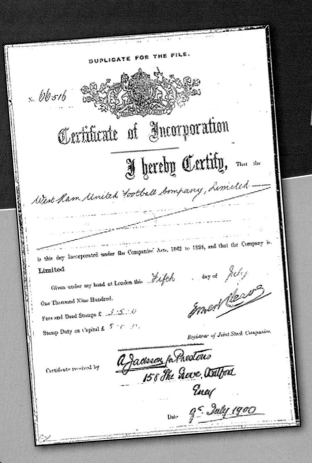

Thames Ironworks owner Arnold Hills offered 4,000, ten-shilling (50p) shares in the new limited company, whose headquarters were based at 55 Barking Road, Canning Town. The philanthropic businessman also offered the use of the Memorial Grounds for a nominal rent for the next three years.

Anticipating the share offer would be under-subscribed, Hills promised to match the sale by buying one for himself for every other one purchased. There was no rush to buy, as a typical east London working man would have been hard-pressed to find the money for even a single share.

The minutes of the first Board meeting reveal that the pioneering board of directors who would supervise the fledgling football club were A. Brown, J.W. Cearns, G.C. Fundell, G.C. Handley, G.J. Hone and C.E. Osborn (chairman).

The directors' first task was to recruit Abraham 'Abe' Norris as trainer at 35 shillings per week (£1.75). A number of the existing players from the Thames Ironworks club were taken on as most were still employed at the shipyard.

The former Ironworks players who would play a part over the coming season were goalkeeper Tommy Moore, defenders Syd King, Charlie Craig, Charlie Dove and George Neil, half-backs Robert Allan and Roderick McEachrane, and forwards Fred Corbett, Frank Taylor and Len Walker.

Walter Tranter, who appeared for the Ironworks between 1896 and 1899, spent one season with Chatham before returning to sign for the Irons.

The minutes also reveal that Scottish and northern recruits such as Hughie Monteith, Jimmy Reid, Luke Raisbeck, Frederick Fenton and William Grassam were each paid their rail fares to attend trial matches arranged for 16 and 23 August 1900, just days before a Southern League fixture kicked-off their new beginnings against Gravesend on 1 September.

The trialists must have impressed Norris as Grassam took just five minutes to score West Ham United's first-ever goal, in front of a crowd of 2,000 at the Memorial Grounds. The flying Scot went on to score four, while a Reid double and one from Fergus Hunt completed a 7-0 drubbing of the Kent side.

The line-up for West Ham United's first match under their modern-day guise was: Monteith, Tranter, Craig, Dove, Raisbeck, McEachrane, Hunt, Grassam, Reid, Kaye and Fenton.

The Irons' first competitive season saw them put together 14 victories against nine defeats, with five matches drawn, securing a sixth-place finish in a League of 15 clubs.

F. King.   E. S. King.   H. Monteith.   C. T. Craig.   F. Hunt.   A. Norris (Trainer).

A. Allan.   J. Bigden.   P. Kyle.   W. Kelly.   R. J. McEachrane.   W. Linward.
W. Grassam.   F. Corbett.   C. W. Ratcliffe.

WEST HAM.   Photographed by J. E. Reeves, Hermit Road, Canning Town.

13 ADRIAN

Born: 3 January 1987, Seville, Spain
Clubs: Real Betis Balompie,
Alcalá (loan), Utrera (loan)
West Ham United Appearances: 68
West Ham United Goals: 0
🐦 @AdriSanMiguel

16

Meet the Management

SLAVEN BILIC

Position: Manager
Born: 11 September 1968, Split, Croatia
Appointed: June 2015

Did you know?

Centre-back Slaven made 54 appearances for West Ham United as a player between February 1996 and May 1997, scoring three goals.

EDIN TERZIC

Position: First-team coach
Born: 30 October 1982, Menden, West Germany
Appointed: July 2015

Did you know?

Edin began his coaching career with German giants Borussia Dortmund, coaching the club's junior sides and working as a scout for manager Jurgen Klopp.

🐦 @edin_terzic

CHRIS WOODS

Position: Goalkeeper coach
Born: 14 November 1959, Swineshead, England
Appointed: July 2015

Did you know?

Chris was capped 43 times by England between 1985 and 1993, travelling to two FIFA World Cup and two UEFA European Championship finals.

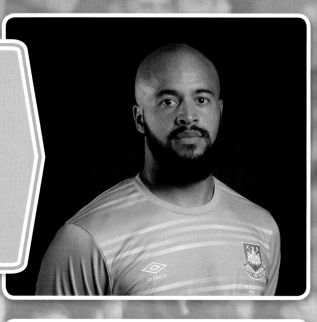

1 DARREN RANDOLPH

Position: Goalkeeper
Born: 12 May 1987, Bray, County Wicklow,
                  Republic of Ireland
Signed from: Birmingham City (June 2015)

Did you know?

Darren was twice voted into the PFA Scotland Team of the Year during three successful seasons with Motherwell.

 @Randz587

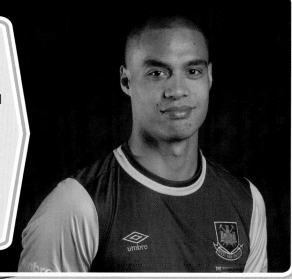

2 WINSTON REID

Position: Centre-back
Born: 3 July 1988, North Shore, Auckland, New Zealand
Signed from: FC Midtjylland (August 2010)

Did you know?

Winston started all three of New Zealand's matches at the 2010 FIFA World Cup in South Africa, scoring in the All Whites' 1-1 draw with Slovakia.

 @WinstonReid2

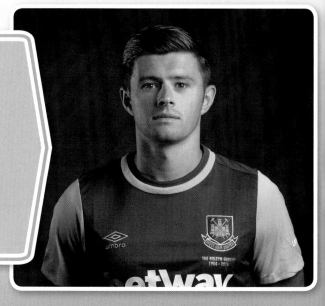

3 AARON CRESSWELL

Position: Left-back
Born: 15 December 1989, Liverpool, England
Signed from: Ipswich Town (July 2014)

Did you know?

Aaron was released by hometown club Liverpool as a schoolboy, before joining Tranmere Rovers and working his way back up to the Premier League.

 @Aaron_Cresswell

4 ALEX SONG

Position: **Deep-lying midfielder**
Born: **9 September 1987, Douala, Cameroon**
Signed from: **FC Barcelona (September 2015)**

Did you know?

Alex is enjoying his second season-long loan spell with West Ham United, having appeared 31 times in Claret and Blue in 2014/15.

@17alexsong

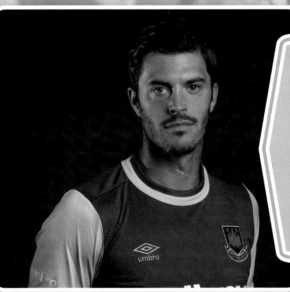

5 JAMES TOMKINS

Position: **Centre-back**
Born: **29 March 1989, Basildon, England**
Signed from: **Academy**

Did you know?

James Tomkins joined West Ham United at the age of seven after being spotted playing for Sunday league club Holy Cross.

 @TomkinsOfficial

8 CHEIKHOU KOUYATE

Position: **Central midfielder**
Born: **21 December 1989, Dakar, Senegal**
Signed from: **RSC Anderlecht (June 2014)**

Did you know?

Cheikhou won four Belgian Pro League titles in the space of five years with RSC Anderlecht between 2010 and 2014.

@PapiCheikhou

Meet the Hammers

9 ANDY CARROLL

Position: Centre forward
Born: 6 January 1989, Gateshead, England
Signed from: Liverpool (May 2013)

Did you know?

Andy scored England's opening goal in the 3-2 group-stage victory over Sweden at UEFA Euro 2012 in Kiev, Ukraine.

 @AndyTCarroll

10 MAURO ZARATE

Position: Forward
Born: 18 March 1987, Haedo, Buenos Aires, Argentina
Signed from: Velez Sarsfield (June 2014)

Did you know?

Mauro is part of a footballing family, as his grandfather Juvenal, father Sergio and brothers Rolando, Ariel and Sergio all played professionally.

 @mau_zeta

11 ENNER VALENCIA

Position: Forward
Born: 4 November 1989, San Lorenzo, Esmeraldas, Ecuador
Signed from: Pachuca (July 2014)

Did you know?

Enner scored three goals for Ecuador at the 2014 FIFA World Cup finals in Brazil – one against Switzerland and two against Honduras.

 @EnnerValencia14

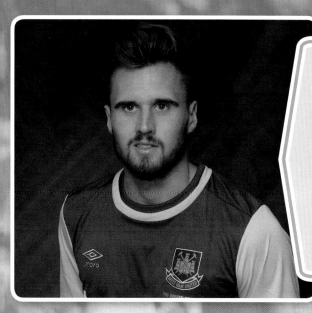

12 CARL JENKINSON

Position: Right-back
Born: 8 February 1992, Harlow, England
Signed from: Arsenal (July 2014)

Did you know?

A full England international Carl also qualified to play for Finland through his mother and appeared once for the Nordic country at Under-21 level in 2011.

13 ADRIAN

Position: Goalkeeper
Born: 3 January 1987, Seville, Spain
Signed from: Real Betis Balompie (July 2013)

Did you know?

Adrian saved three consecutive Premier League penalties in spring 2015, from Tottenham Hotspur's Harry Kane, Leicester City's David Nugent and Queens Park Rangers' Charlie Austin.

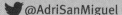 @AdriSanMiguel

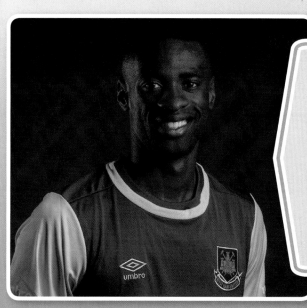

14 PEDRO OBIANG

Position: Deep-lying midfielder
Born: 27 March 1992, Alcalá de Henares, Spain
Signed from: UC Sampdoria (July 2015)

Did you know?

Pedro's home city of Alcalá de Henares – meaning Citadel on the river Henares – in central Spain is one of UNESCO's World Heritage Sites due to its rich archaeology.

 @Obiang14

15 DIAFRA SAKHO

Position: Centre-forward
Born: 24 December 1989, Guédiawaye, Senegal
Signed from: FC Metz (August 2014)

Did you know?
Diafra was voted France's Ligue 2 Player of the Year after leading FC Metz to promotion in 2013/14.

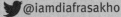 @iamdiafrasakho

16 MARK NOBLE

Position: Central midfielder
Born: 8 May 1987, Canning Town, England
Signed from: Academy

Did you know?
Mark has made more Premier League appearances for West Ham United than any other player.

 @Noble16Mark

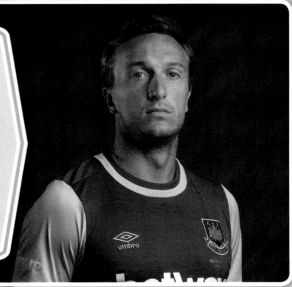

17 JOEY O'BRIEN

Position: Full-back
Born: 17 February 1986, Dublin, Republic of Ireland
Signed from: Bolton Wanderers (July 2011)

Did you know?
Joey O'Brien had a trial with West Ham United as a schoolboy before joining Bolton Wanderers at the age of 16.

18 MORGAN AMALFITANO

Position: Wide midfielder
Born: 20 March 1985, Nice, France
Signed from: Olympique de Marseille (September 2014)

Did you know?

Morgan set up the winning goal on his France debut in a 2-1 victory over Germany in Bremen in February 2012.

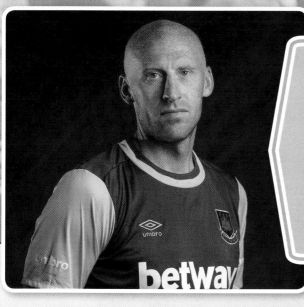

19 JAMES COLLINS

Position: Centre-back
Born: 23 August 1983, Newport, Wales
Signed from: Aston Villa (August 2012)

Did you know?

James is in his second spell with West Ham United, having scored twice in 65 appearances between 2005 and 2009.

@gingercollins19

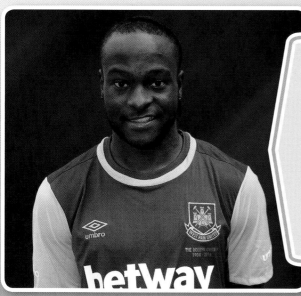

20 VICTOR MOSES

Position: Winger
Born: 12 December 1990, Kaduna, Nigeria
Signed from: Chelsea (September 2015)

Did you know?

Victor Moses helped Nigeria to win the CAF Africa Cup of Nations title in 2013, scoring twice and being named in the Team of the Tournament.

 @VictorMoses

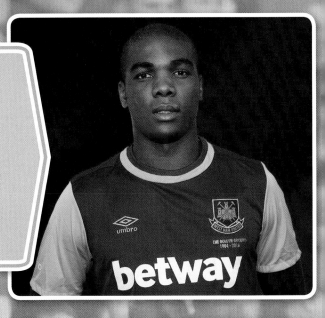

21 ANGELO OGBONNA

Position: Centre-back
Born: 23 May 1988, Cassino, Italy
Signed from: Juventus (July 2015)

Did you know?

Angelo won two Serie A titles, the Italian Cup and Italian Super Cup during two successful seasons with Juventus.

 @OgbonnaOfficial

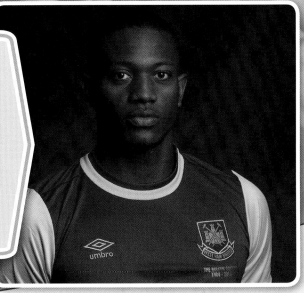

25 DONEIL HENRY

Position: Centre-back
Born: 20 April 1993, Brampton, Ontario, Canada
Signed from: Apollon Limassol (January 2015)

Did you know?

Doneil won three consecutive Canadian Championship titles with Toronto FC in 2010, 2011 and 2012.

26 NIKICA JELAVIC

Position: Centre forward
Born: 27 August 1985, apljina, SFR Yugoslavia
Signed from: Hull City (September 2015)

Did you know?

Nikica Jelavic was handed his international debut by Slaven Bilic, scoring on his first appearance for Croatia against Qatar in Rijeka on 8 October 2009.

27 DIMITRI PAYET

Position: Attacking midfielder
Born: 29 March 1987, Saint-Pierre, Réunion, France
Signed from: Olympique de Marseille (June 2015)

Did you know?

Dimitri was voted into France's Ligue 1 Team of the Year in both 2012/13 and 2014/15.

🐦 @dimpayet17

28 MANUEL LANZINI

Position: Attacking midfielder
Born: 15 February 1993, Ituzaingó, Argentina
Signed from: Al Jazira Club (July 2015)

Did you know?

Manuel came through the same River Plate youth system as the likes of former Hammer Javier Mascherano, Ariel Ortega and Alfredo Di Stefano.

🐦 @maanuulanzini10

30 MICHAIL ANTONIO

Position: Winger
Born: 28 March 1990, Wandsworth, London, England
Signed from: Nottingham Forest (September 2015)

Did you know?

Michail Antonio has progressed from the Isthmian League to the Premier League, having started his career with Tooting & Mitcham United.

🐦 @Michailantonio

32 REECE BURKE

Position: Centre-back
Born: 2 September 1996, Newham, England
Signed from: Academy

Did you know?
Reece Burke made his West Ham United debut in an FA Cup tie at Nottingham Forest in January 2014 at the age of 17 years and four months.

@reeceburke5

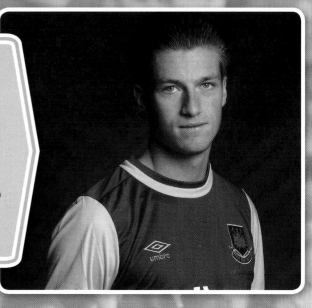

33 STEPHEN HENDRIE

Position: Left-back
Born: 8 January 1995, Glasgow, Scotland
Signed from: Hamilton Academical (July 2015)

Did you know?
Stephen has been capped by his native Scotland at U17, U19 and U21 levels.

@HendrieStephen

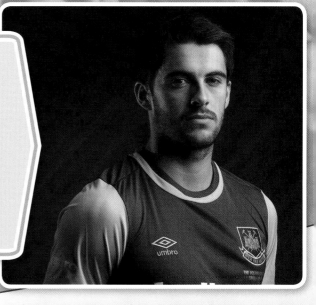

34 RAPHAEL SPIEGEL

Position: Goalkeeper
Born: 19 December 1992, Rüttenen, Switzerland
Signed from: Grasshopper (July 2012)

Did you know?
Raphael was part of the Switzerland squad which won the FIFA U-17 World Cup in 2009.

@_speeks_

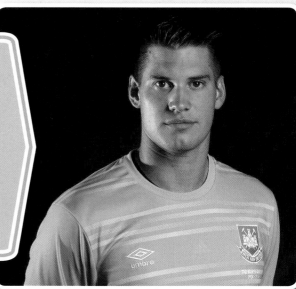

35 REECE OXFORD

Position: Centre-half
Born: 16 December 1998, Edmonton, London, England
Signed from: Academy

Did you know?

Reece became West Ham United's youngest-ever player when he debuted against FC Lusitans in the UEFA Europa League on 2 July 2015.

 @Reeceoxford_

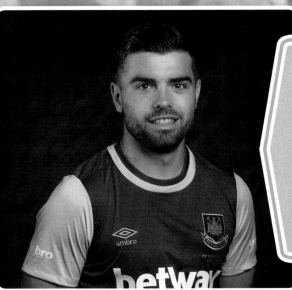

36 ELLIOT LEE

Position: Striker
Born: 16 December 1994, Durham, England
Signed from: Academy

Did you know?

Elliot Lee is the son of former Newcastle United, West Ham United and England midfielder Rob Lee.

 @elliotlee9

42 MARTIN SAMUELSEN

Position: Winger
Born: 17 April 1997, Haugesund, Norway
Signed from: Manchester City (June 2015)

Did you know?

Martin has been capped by Norway at U16, U17 and U18 levels.

 @samuelseen

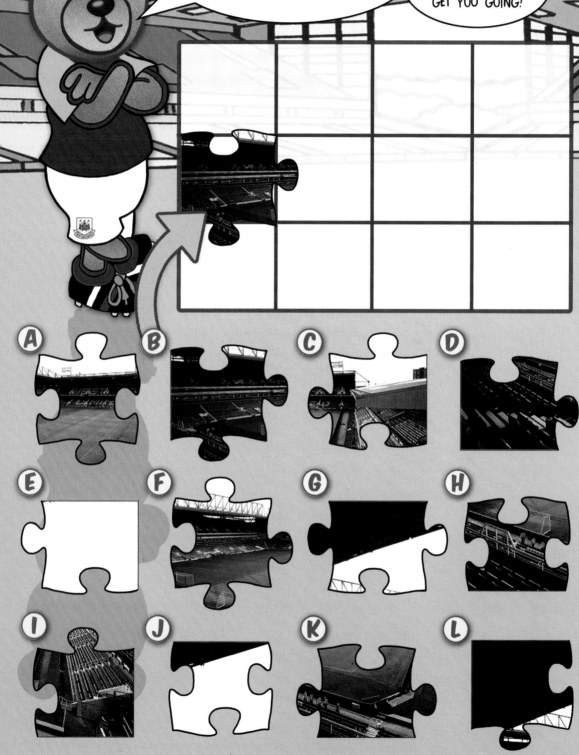

Boleyn BLAST FROM THE PAST

During a Premier League fixture in February 2000, Paolo Di Canio and Frank Lampard couldn't decide which one of them should take a penalty.

BUT MY UNCLE SAYS I TAKE PENALTIES!

1. Who eventually took (and scored) the penalty?

A: Frank Lampard   B: Paolo Di Canio
C: Neither of them!

2. Who was our opposition that day?

A: Leicester City   B: Bradford City   C: Hull City

3. What was the final score?

A: 3-2 to West Ham   B: 4-3 to West Ham
C: 5-4 to West Ham

HAMMERHEAD'S LOOKALIKEY

ARSENAL'S DANNY WELBECK

A YAWNING TORTOISE

CAN YOU NAME THE THREE CLUB GREATS THIS FACE IS MADE UP OF?

PLAYER 1: _____
PLAYER 2: _____
PLAYER 3: _____

Answers:

Boleyn Blast from the Past:
1. (B) Paolo Di Canio
2. (B) Bradford City 3. (C) 5-4

Boleyn Ground Jigsaw (left):
Top Row: L, G, J, E
Middle Row: B, F, A, C
Bottom Row: D, H, K, I

The face is made up of...
1. John Hartson (top)
2. Slaven Bilic (middle) and
3. Carlos Tevez (bottom)

Boleyn Ground by Numbers

A numerical look back at the history of West Ham United's historic home

Number of London Underground lines serving Upton Park station – Metropolitan and Hammersmith & City.

2

3

Number of senior international matches played at the Boleyn Ground – England v Australia (2003), Italy v Ivory Coast (2010) and Argentina v Croatia (2014).

70

Number of Executive Boxes at the Boleyn Ground, including one luxury Penthouse Suite on the halfway line in the Betway Stand.

8

The highest number of goals West Ham United scored in a single league match – a feat the Hammers have achieved three times.

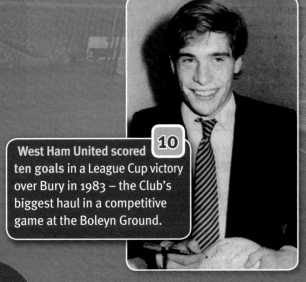

10

West Ham United scored ten goals in a League Cup victory over Bury in 1983 – the Club's biggest haul in a competitive game at the Boleyn Ground.

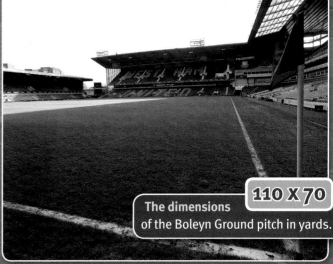

110 X 70

The dimensions of the Boleyn Ground pitch in yards.

112 The number of seasons West Ham United have spent at the Boleyn Ground.

1904 The year West Ham United moved into the Boleyn Ground, beating Millwall 3-0 in their opening Southern League First Division fixture on 1 September.

1944 The year in which a German V-1 flying bomb landed on the Boleyn Ground, destroying the Club offices and causing major damage to the south-west corner of the stadium and pitch.

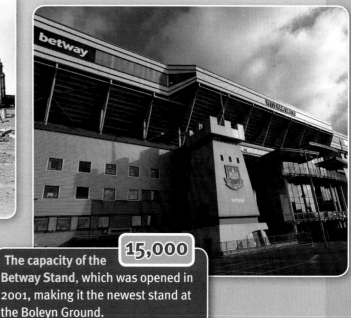

15,000 The capacity of the Betway Stand, which was opened in 2001, making it the newest stand at the Boleyn Ground.

35,016 The capacity of the Boleyn Ground in its final season in existence – 2015/16.

HAMMER
THE OFFICIAL PROGRAMME OF
WEST HAM UNITED

1970-71

TOTTENHAM HOTSPUR
FOOTBALL LEAGUE: FIRST DIVISION
Saturday 17 October 1970 at 3 pm

G (5p.)   17

42,322 The record home league attendance for a West Ham United fixture at the Boleyn Ground, achieved for the 2-2 Division One draw with Tottenham Hotspur on 17 October 1970.

44,232 The record attendance at the Boleyn Ground, achieved against Birmingham in an FA Cup sixth round tie on 4 March 1933.

My Matchday

Young Hammer of the Year Reece Burke takes you through his typical home matchday

West Ham United footballers prepare long and hard for every single match, physically and mentally.

However, each player has his own habits, routines and superstitions which he will stick to in order to maximise his level of performance come 3pm on a Saturday afternoon.

Here, Young Hammer of the Year Reece Burke takes you through his typical home matchday.

What time do you get up on a matchday?

I don't get up at a set time on a Saturday. It depends to be honest, I usually like a lie in so I get up when I get up. It's important to be well rested before a match. The day before a game, you ideally want eight to nine hours sleep to make sure you're mentally strong. Obviously, if you're tired then your concentration levels aren't quite there.

So, I have a good night's sleep and wake up fairly early. They say breakfast is the most important meal of the day so after I wake up, I'll go downstairs and have breakfast. I usually have scrambled eggs on toast.

For a 3pm kick off, we're told to get to the ground for 11.45am. Once we arrive we have a pre-match meal which is usually chicken and pasta. After that it's all about preparing for the game.

Are you a player who likes to bring their own boots or kit or does the kit man do it all?

Sometimes I take my own boots but usually, if the kit man is willing, I'll let him take them. He's a busy man with everyone's stuff to look after.

32

What happens if your family come to a game, do you arrange tickets for them?

Yes, always! Coming up to a game, if I feel like I might be involved or if I'm told I'm on the teamsheet then I always make sure I get tickets. My Mum and Dad always turn up and my sister does as often as possible. I always make sure I get at least three tickets and then sometimes more for other friends or family.

After a pre-match meal, what do you do next?

Before we go out to warm-up on the pitch, we do a lot of stretching. We go through a routine called activation where you begin to stretch and prepare physically for the game. It's obviously vital to get your body ready for the game.

We normally go out about 35 minutes before kick-off. It's important to get moving and warmed up for the game. About ten minutes or so before kick-off we come in for some final prep, I put my shin-pads on and any tape or strappings.

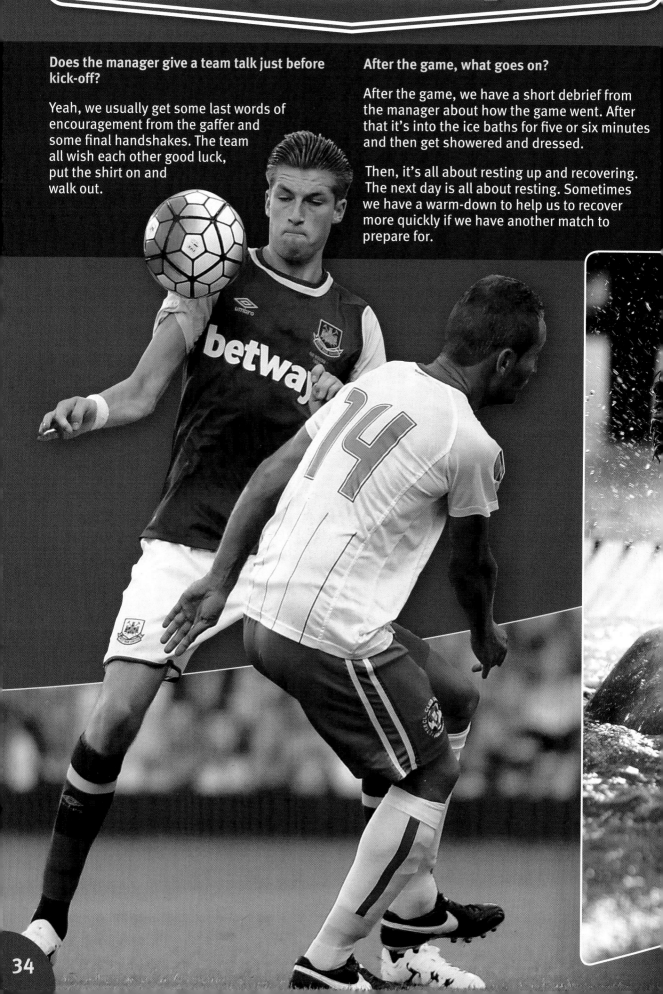

Does the manager give a team talk just before kick-off?

Yeah, we usually get some last words of encouragement from the gaffer and some final handshakes. The team all wish each other good luck, put the shirt on and walk out.

After the game, what goes on?

After the game, we have a short debrief from the manager about how the game went. After that it's into the ice baths for five or six minutes and then get showered and dressed.

Then, it's all about resting up and recovering. The next day is all about resting. Sometimes we have a warm-down to help us to recover more quickly if we have another match to prepare for.

When do you see your family?

After getting dressed I see my family first. They're usually in the Players' Lounge or a box upstairs. It's always nice to see them, they're at every game and they're very proud.

Sometimes you have a bit of media to do. Do you feel like you've got used to that now?

At first I wouldn't say I was great but I think I'm getting better at that side of things. The more you do the easier it gets. I used to sometimes try and hide or run away! Now, it's all good and it's part of being a professional player.

After that, home to relax? Or do you watch the game back or sit down for Match of the Day?

It depends on the how the match has gone. You always replay the game in your head on the way home. Thankfully more often than not I've had good experiences, but the bad moments do linger sometimes.

I actually think it's the bad games that make you a good player because you don't learn as much from the good games. You have to make sure that you learn from any mistakes and bounce back from them.

The next day, I'll watch the game back and do the homework on it. I remember watching the Nottingham Forest game back, that was a steep learning curve but I think I've improved a lot because of it.

Spot the Difference

Can you spot the ten differences between the two images of manager Slaven Bilic greeting players inside the West Ham United dressing room?

Answers can be found on page 61!

AUTOGRAPH:

ADRIÁN

 DEBUT: 27TH AUGUST 2013
POSITION: GOALKEEPER
COUNTRY: SPAIN

Boleyn Ground A-Z

An alphabetical journey through the history of
West Ham United's historic home of 111 years

A is for Attendance – The highest official attendance for a Boleyn Ground fixture is the 44,232 who turned up to see West Ham United beat Birmingham City 4-0 in an FA Cup quarter-final on 4 March 1933.

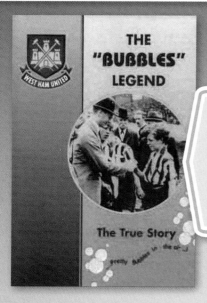

THE "BUBBLES" LEGEND

The True Story

B is for Bubbles – West Ham United fans have been singing the Club's anthem I'm Forever Blowing Bubbles since the 1920s, when the song was used in a soap advert featuring a child who looked like West Ham Boys player Will Murray.

C is for Chicken Run – The Chicken Run was a terrace that ran along the length of the old East Stand until the structure was demolished in the summer of 1968. It was given its unusual name due to its appearance, with a terrace covered by a corrugated iron roof and chicken wire used to contain supporters.

D is for Defeat – West Ham United's record defeat at the Boleyn Ground was an 8-2 First Division thrashing by Blackburn Rovers on Boxing Day 1963. Two days later, the Hammers travelled to Ewood Park for the reverse fixture and won 3-1!

E is for East Stand – The oldest and smallest stand at the Boleyn Ground, the East Stand was built in 1969 and houses just 5,000 supporters in two tiers.

F is for Fans – The Boleyn Ground has been visited by millions of fans in its 111-year existence, including the 662,552 who watched West Ham United's 19 Barclays Premier League matches in 2014/15.

G is for Green Street – Green Street is the road on which the Boleyn Ground sits. It has existed since the 15th century as the boundary of the ancient parishes of East Ham and West Ham.

H is for House – Green Street House was built in the mid-16th century and later became known as Boleyn Castle, following suggestions that Anne Boleyn had lived there and due to its castle-like appearance. It later became a Roman Catholic School and was demolished in 1955.

I is for International – The Boleyn Ground has hosted three senior international matches – England versus Australia in 2003, Italy versus Ivory Coast in August 2010 and Argentina versus Croatia in November 2014.

J is for John Lyall Gates – The John Lyall Gates have been situated at the main entrance to the Boleyn Ground since 1956 and were renamed in honour of the late West Ham United manager in December 2009.

K is for Knockout – The Boleyn Ground has hosted a number of boxing cards in recent years, including bouts involving West Ham United fans Kevin Mitchell and Danny Williams.

L is for Logo – The West Ham United logo – or crest – is emblazoned on the pitch surround at the mouth of the Boleyn Ground tunnel. This logo will be replaced by a new design in summer 2016.

M is for Mission – In 1989, the American evangelist Billy Graham held a three-day mission to London, part of which was held at the Boleyn Ground.

N is for Newham – The Boleyn Ground is situated in the London Borough of Newham, which was formed by merging the former area of the Essex county borough of East Ham and the county borough of West Ham as a borough of the newly formed Greater London on 1 April 1965.

Newham London

O is for Olympic Stadium – West Ham United will move to the converted 54,000-capacity UEFA Category 4 London 2012 Olympic Stadium in Stratford in summer 2016.

P is for Pitch – The pitch dimensions at the Boleyn Ground are 100.58m x 68m, making it one of the shortest in the Barclays Premier League.

Q is for Queen – HM Queen Elizabeth II and Prince Philip, Duke of Edinburgh visited the Boleyn Ground in 2001 to open the redeveloped West Stand, which can hold up to 15,000 supporters.

R is for Record Win – West Ham United have twice won 8-0 in Football League matches – against Rotherham United in the Second Division in March 1958 and Sunderland in the First Division in October 1968.

S is for South Bank – The South Bank was a large terrace which could hold 9,400 supporters. It was initially uncovered before a roof was placed over the stand in 1953. It was demolished in 1991 and replaced by the all-seater Bobby Moore Stand.

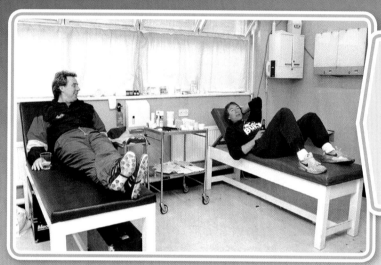

T is for Treatment Room – The Treatment Room is where players – and staff – will go to receive massages, therapies and strappings before kick-off, and where they will be treated for non-serious injuries suffered during the match itself.

U is for Upton Park – The Boleyn Ground is commonly called Upton Park by supporters and pundits alike. Upton Park is in fact the area of London centred around Green Street where the stadium is situated.

V is for V-1 flying bomb – A German V-1 rocket-propelled flying bomb landed on the south-west corner of the pitch in August 1944, causing severe damage to the ground, while the resulting fire gutted the Club's offices and destroyed historical records and documents.

W is for World Cup – Four 1966 FIFA World Cup winners – West Ham United trio Bobby Moore, Geoff Hurst and Martin Peters and Everton's Ray Wilson – are depicted holding the Jules Rimet Trophy aloft in a sculpture situated on the junction of Green Street and Barking Road.

HAMMER

1972 1973

THE OFFICIAL PROGRAMME OF
WEST HAM UNITED

ISRAEL NATIONAL XI
PAUL HEFFER TESTIMONIAL MATCH
Wednesday 4 April 1973 at 7.30 p.m.
TWOPENCE

X is for XI – West Ham United hosted an Israeli XI in Paul Heffer's Testimonial match on 4 April 1973, with the game ending in a 3-2 win for the Hammers.

Y is for Youth Cup – The second leg of the 1999 FA Youth Cup final saw an estimated 25,000 fans turn out to see a West Ham United team containing Michael Carrick and Joe Cole thrash Coventry City 6-0 to complete a 9-0 aggregate success. The Hammers have won the competition on two other occasions, in 1963 and 1981.

Z is for Zola – Gianfranco Zola became West Ham United's first non-British manager when he was appointed in September 2008. The former Italy star spent two seasons in charge at the Boleyn Ground.

Pre-Season

West Ham United travelled far and wide as Sam Allardyce prepared his squad for the 2014/15 Barclays Premier League campaign.

After kicking-off pre-season with draws at Stevenage and Ipswich Town, the Hammers jetted to the other side of the world for the four-team Football United Tour tournament in New Zealand.

There, West Ham took on A-League sides Wellington Phoenix and Sydney FC, and made many new friends at a host of events and appearances, ranging from a traditional Maori welcome to regular open training sessions in Auckland and Wellington.

After a short period at home, the squad headed to Germany for the Schalke 04 Cup, where they faced the host club and Spanish side Malaga.

Pre-season ended with a memorable moment for Academy aces Elliot Lee and Reece Burke as they combined for the latter to net the winner in a 3-2 Marathonbet Cup victory over Italian outfit Sampdoria.

August

The Hammers went into the 2014/15 season in a confident mood and produced a fine opening-day Barclays Premier League display against Tottenham Hotspur at the Boleyn Ground, only for Mark Noble's missed penalty and Eric Dier's last-gasp goal to condemn the hosts to defeat.

West Ham bounced back to form with a fantastic 3-1 victory at Crystal Palace, with Mauro Zarate and Stewart Downing scoring beauties.

Diafra Sakho then marked his first start with a wonderful header against Sheffield United, only for the Blades to knock the home side out of the Capital One Cup on penalties.

The opening month of the campaign ended with another disappointing defeat at the Boleyn Ground, this time in the Barclays Premier League at the hands of Ronald Koeman's high-flying Southampton.

September

West Ham United's rollercoaster season was seen in microcosm in September, when the Hammers took part in a thrilling draw, pulled off a stunning win and suffered a frustrating defeat.

The transfer window closed with the Hammers having enjoyed a productive summer in the market, bringing in no fewer than eight new players – Aaron Cresswell, Diafra Sakho, Cheikhou Kouyate, Enner Valencia, Diego Poyet, loanees Alex Song and Carl Jenkinson and deadline day signing Morgan Amalfitano.

All eight would play their part over the coming months, but it was strike partners Valencia and Sakho who made their mark first, scoring in a 2-2 draw at Hull City. The Ecuador forward thumped in an unstoppable 25-yarder to announce his arrival in English football before Sakho scored a late equaliser.

Next up came Liverpool, with Winston Reid, Sakho and Amalfitano scoring in a 3-1 home win, before the Senegalese striker netted for a fourth straight start, in a narrow 2-1 defeat at Manchester United.

October

As summer turned to autumn, West Ham's form turned as red hot as the leaves on the trees.

First, Championship Play-Off winners Queens Park Rangers were beaten 2-0 at the Boleyn Ground, with one from the prolific Sakho and a Nedum Onuoha own-goal doing the business.

The No15 was on target again in a 3-1 win at fellow new boys Burnley, with Valencia also scoring with a world-class long-range header and Carlton Cole netting his second of the campaign to secure the victory.

A perfect tenth month of the year was complete with the best victory of the three – a 2-1 home win over champions Manchester City, courtesy of Amalfitano's close-range finish and Sakho's pinpoint header.

November

West Ham United's outstanding October was followed by a decent November.

Five points from four matches may not look like a particularly good return, but it could so easily have been many more.

The month began with a trip to the Britannia Stadium, where Stok City raced into a two-goal lead early in the second half. However, these Hammers were made of stern stuff and, inspired by the outstanding Stewart Downing, clawed their way level by full-time.

A week later, struggling Aston Villa were the visitors. Andy Carroll made a welcome return from injury as a late substitute and came within a whisker of winning it for the hosts, only for Brad Guzan's heroics to earn the visitors a goalless draw.

A narrow 2-1 defeat at Everton was followed by a fine 1-0 home victory over Newcastle United, with the winner coming courtesy of Aaron Cresswell's first goal for the Club.

December

Six matches were played in the final month of 2014, with West Ham initially continuing their magnificent start to the campaign to climb into the top-four come Christmas Day.

December started with a trip to The Hawthorns, where Kevin Nolan's 99th league goal and a James Tomkins header secured a 2-1 win.

Next up, Carroll continued his one-man crusade against Swansea City by scoring two fine headers in a 3-1 win, with Sakho adding a thumping late third, before Stewart Downing's effort secured a 1-1 draw at Sunderland.

Leicester City put up a brave fight in the final game before Christmas, but goals from Carroll and Downing did the business.

The year ended on a down note, though, as back-to-back defeats at home to Arsenal and at Chelsea finally threatened to burst West Ham's bubble.

January

The New Year kicked-off with a visit from West Bromwich Albion to the Boleyn Ground, and the relegation-threatened Baggies worked hard to secure a deserved 1-1 draw.

Next up came an FA Cup third-round trip to Everton, where Romelu Lukaku's late leveller forced a replay.

A third straight 1-1 draw was secured at Swansea City, where Andy Carroll scored a truly wonderful individual goal.

A goalless first half suggested little of the drama to follow in the FA Cup replay with Everton, but the tie exploded after the break. Enner Valencia scored, Aiden McGeady was sent-off and Kevin Mirallas equalised to force extra-time. Lukaku scored, Carlton Cole levelled and Adrian downed gloves before putting West Ham through 9-8 on penalties in a true classic.

A routine 3-0 home win over Hull City was followed by a hard-fought FA Cup fourth-round win at League One champions-elect Bristol City, but Liverpool proved too strong in the month's final league fixture.

February

February was a month of frustrating last-gasp levellers for the Hammers.

First, Manchester United snatched an undeserved point at the Boleyn Ground, when Daley Blind cancelled out Cheikhou Kouyate's wonderful volleyed strike.

A heroic goalless draw at Southampton was ruined by Andy Carroll's serious knee injury, and the misery deepened when West Bromwich Albion ended West Ham's FA Cup dreams with a 4-0 thrashing at The Hawthorns.

West Ham bounced back from that horror show to go 2-0 up at Tottenham Hotspur through Kouyate and compatriot Diafra Sakho, only for two late goals to deny the visitors another famous win at White Hart Lane.

Alan Pardew's second return of the season came with Crystal Palace on 28 February, with the resurgent Eagles soaring to a 3-1 victory in east London.

March

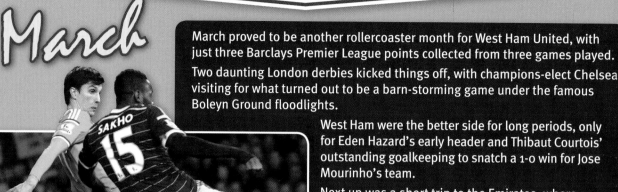

March proved to be another rollercoaster month for West Ham United, with just three Barclays Premier League points collected from three games played.

Two daunting London derbies kicked things off, with champions-elect Chelsea visiting for what turned out to be a barn-storming game under the famous Boleyn Ground floodlights.

West Ham were the better side for long periods, only for Eden Hazard's early header and Thibaut Courtois' outstanding goalkeeping to snatch a 1-0 win for Jose Mourinho's team.

Next up was a short trip to the Emirates, where Arsenal proved too strong to prevail 3-0, but West Ham would avoid a second winless month in succession by defeating a struggling Sunderland.

Diafra Sakho kept his head to steer the ball into the bottom left-hand corner after good work from January loan signing Nene and Mark Noble, sending the Black Cats to an agonising 1-0 loss.

April

Frustrating and injury-affected were the two adjectives that best summed up the month.

In theory, West Ham United were set fair for a productive April, with fixtures against two relegation-threatened sides and a home game against mid-table Stoke City.

Unfortunately, it did not play out that way, with James Tomkins (dislocated shoulder), Diafra Sakho (thigh), Andy Carroll (knee) and Winston Reid (hamstring) and Alex Song (back) all missing all or some of the four matches through injury.

Leicester City kick-started their renaissance through Andy King's late winner at the King Power Stadium, before Marko Arnautovic's last-gasp equaliser scored Stoke a 1-1 draw in east London.

Next up came another fruitless trip to the Etihad, where Manchester City notched a comfortable 2-0 win, before the month rounded out with a third Adrian penalty save in succession in a goalless draw at lowly Queens Park Rangers.

May

West Ham United endured a May that will not live long in the memory of Hammers fans.

As the final month of the season began, Sam Allardyce's side had dropped into the bottom half of the Barclays Premier League table for the first time since September.

Mark Noble's first-half penalty saw off the challenge of a desperate Burnley side who would end the campaign by being relegated back to the Championship.

That Boleyn Ground win would see West Ham collect their final points of the season, as Big Sam's side stumbled to defeats at Aston Villa (0-1) at home to Everton (1-2) and away to Newcastle United (0-2) to complete a desperate second half to 2014/15.

The Hammers finished a season that promised more in 12th place. Allardyce and the Club announced a parting of ways shortly after the final whistle at St James' Park, bringing down the curtain on his four-year spell in charge.

50

2014-15 SEASON REVIEW

Off The Pitch

Away from the pitch – and the outstanding work being carried out to transform West Ham United's new home – it has been an eventful season in east London.

A host of new high-profile sponsors and partners have joined forces with West Ham throughout the campaign, marking the Hammers' continuing expansion and development as one of English football's leading Clubs.

In February, West Ham appointed Betway as the Club's new principal sponsor, while Umbro were confirmed as the Club's new technical partner as recently as 30 April.

In addition, adidas, Spire Roding Healthcare, Lycamobile, Marathonbet, ICU Label, Carlsberg, Apsley Tailors, Winner.co.uk, Mondogoal and Playvideo have all shown their support to the Club as valued partners throughout 2014/15.

Charity-wise, West Ham are principal partners in the recently-launched Moore Family Foundation and DT38 – founded in memory of the late West Ham striker Dylan Tombides. The Bobby Moore Fund for Cancer Research UK and Richard House Hospice also receive continued support, as do campaigns including Football vs Homophobia, Kick It Out, Show Racism The Red Card, Prostate Cancer UK, MS-UK, Football Fighting Ebola and Know The Score.

Aside from attending a wide variety of charity, sponsor and partner events, the first-team squad have also

made their positive presence felt during visits to local hospitals and hospices, hosted training ground visits and dropped in to surprise unwitting supporters with tickets, kits and more.

On top of all that, the players have been out and about regularly at Store signings, fan forums and all manner of community events.

With regular visits made to check on the work going on in Stratford, it has been a non-stop season off the pitch, with the Club's bright future only set to see the schedule become even busier next term.

27 DIMITRI PAYET

Born: 29 March 1987, Saint-Pierre, Reunion, France

Clubs: Nantes, St-Etienne, Lille, Marseille, West Ham United

France Caps: 15

France Goals: 1

🐦 @dimpayet17

AUTOGRAPH:

WEST HAM UNITED

AARON CRESSWELL

DEBUT: 16TH AUGUST 2014
POSITION: DEFENDER
COUNTRY: ENGLAND

54

3 AARON CRESSWELL

Born: 15 September 1989, Liverpool, England
Clubs: Tranmere Rovers, Ipswich Town
West Ham United Appearances: 42
West Ham United Goals: 2
@Aaron_Cresswell

55

ONCE YOU HAVE FOUND ALL THE GROUNDS IN HAMMERHEAD'S GRID, LINK THEM UP TO THE TEAM THAT PLAY THEIR HOME GAMES THERE!

ALL ANSWERS AT THE BOTTOM OF THE PAGE!

- ANFIELD
- BOLEYN GROUND
- BRITANNIA STADIUM
- CARROW ROAD
- EMIRATES STADIUM
- ETIHAD STADIUM
- GOODISON PARK
- KING POWER STADIUM
- LIBERTY STADIUM
- OLD TRAFFORD
- SELHURST PARK
- STADIUM OF LIGHT
- STAMFORD BRIDGE
- ST JAMES' PARK
- ST MARY'S STADIUM
- THE HAWTHORNS
- VICARAGE ROAD
- VILLA PARK
- VITALITY STADIUM
- WHITE HART LANE

- AFC BOURNEMOUTH
- ARSENAL
- ASTON VILLA
- CHELSEA
- CRYSTAL PALACE
- EVERTON
- LEICESTER CITY
- LIVERPOOL
- MANCHESTER CITY
- MANCHESTER UNITED
- NEWCASTLE UNITED
- NORWICH CITY
- SOUTHAMPTON
- STOKE CITY
- SUNDERLAND
- SWANSEA CITY
- TOTTENHAM HOTSPUR
- WATFORD
- WEST BROMWICH ALBION
- WEST HAM UNITED

MYSTERY MAN

Clue 1: I was born in 1992.
Clue 2: I have played for Spain U21s.
Clue 3: My last club was Sampdoria in Italy.

The mystery Hammer is

_____

BUBBLES' TRICKY TEASER

Which current Hammer has played for these three French clubs?

Marseille

Saint-Étienne

LILLE LOSC
Lille

The player is _____

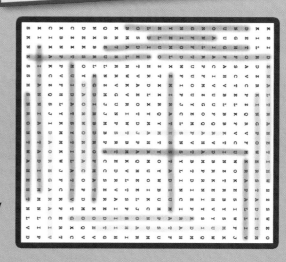

Mystery Man: Pedro Obiang
Bubbles' Tricky Teaser: Dimitri Payet.
Anfield - Liverpool. Boleyn Ground - West Ham United.
Britannia Stadium - Stoke City. Carrow Road - Norwich City. Emirates Stadium -
Arsenal. Etihad Stadium - Manchester City. Goodison Park - Everton. King Power
Stadium - Leicester City. Old Trafford - Manchester United. Selhurst Park -
Crystal Palace. Stadium of Light - Sunderland. Stamford Bridge - Chelsea.
St James' Park - Newcastle United. St Mary's Stadium - Southampton.
The Hawthorns - West Bromwich Albion. Vicarage Road - Watford.
Villa Park - Aston Villa. Vitality Stadium - AFC Bournemouth.
White Hart Lane - Tottenham Hotspur.

Greatest Matches

Thousands of matches have been played on the hallowed turf at the Boleyn Ground since West Ham United moved into the stadium in 1904.

Bury were smashed 10-0 in a League Cup tie in 1983, while Rotherham United and Sunderland have been hammered 8-0 and Arsenal were hit for seven.

However, when asked to nominate their favourite matches in Boleyn Ground history, the following five finished top of the voting!

Number 1

West Ham United 3 Eintracht Frankfurt 1

European Cup Winners' Cup semi-final second leg, 14 April 1976

West Ham United welcomed West German Cup holders Eintracht Frankfurt to east London for the second leg of their European Cup Winners' Cup tie, trailing 2-1 from the first meeting.

In relentless rain and on a bumpy pitch, West Ham took the lead after half-time when Trevor Brooking headed Frank Lampard's cross over the goalkeeper.

Keith Robson then curled the Hammers into a two-goal lead from 25 yards before Brooking added his second of the night with superb control and a low finish, rendering the Germans' late consolation goal meaningless.

On an incredible night topped by an unrivalled Boleyn Ground atmosphere, John Lyall's side reached the Club's second European Cup Winners' Cup final.

Unfortunately, there the Belgian side RSC Anderlecht would prove too strong and run out 4-2 winners in their home city of Brussels.

Number 2

West Ham United 7 Leeds United 0

League Cup fourth round, 7 November 1966

Don Revie's Leeds United were one of the top teams in the country when they visited the Boleyn Ground on the evening of Monday 7 November 1966.

Four months removed from England's FIFA World Cup success, Leeds boasted international defenders Jack Charlton and Norman Hunter.

No matter, though, as Ron Greenwood's West Ham included England captain Bobby Moore, outstanding midfielder Martin Peters and goal scorer supreme Geoff Hurst.

It was young winger John Sissons who took centre-stage initially, though, bagging a first-half hat-trick before Hurst made it 4-0 before half-time.

Into the second period and Leeds were put to the sword as Hurst completed his hat-trick either side of a goal from fellow Three Lions hero Peters.

Number 3

West Ham United 5 Bradford City 4

Premier League, 12 February 2000

The Hammers triumphed in a nine-goal epic on one of the craziest afternoons ever witnessed at the Boleyn Ground.

Harry Redknapp's side looked down and out when they trailed 4-2 with just 25 minutes remaining, only for Frank Lampard's late goal to turn a topsy-turvy game in West Ham's favour once and for all.

After a goalless opening half-hour, Bradford went ahead before Trevor Sinclair and John Moncur scored and Peter Beagrie levelled it at 2-2 a minute before half-time.

Jamie Lawrence's quickfire brace appeared to have condemned West Ham to an embarrassing home defeat before Paolo Di Canio wrestled the ball from Lampard to pull one back from the penalty spot.

Joe Cole then equalised before Lampard completed an amazing match with an 83rd-minute winner.

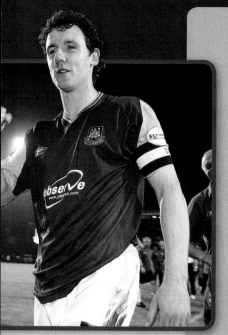

Number 4

West Ham United 2 Ipswich Town 0

Division One Play-Off semi-final second leg, 18 May 2004

Nobody who was inside the Boleyn Ground on the night of Tuesday 18 May 2004 will ever forget the cauldron-like atmosphere which roared West Ham United through to the Division One Play-Off final.

With 34,002 fans packed inside the stadium, the Hammers overcame a 1-0 first leg deficit to defeat a shell-shocked Ipswich Town 2-0 on the night and 2-1 on aggregate.

Steve Lomas, Bobby Zamora and Christian Dailly all went close in the first half before winger Matty Etherington broke the deadlock with an outstanding strike five minutes after half-time.

With the ground literally shaking and the noise deafening, striker David Connolly then missed a great chance to put West Ham further ahead before Ipswich's Ian Westlake hit a post.

It mattered not, however, as the unlikely figure of the curly-haired Dailly fired home via a deflection to book West Ham's passage to Cardiff's Millennium Stadium.

Number 5

West Ham United 4 Manchester United 0

League Cup quarter-final, 30 November 2010

West Ham United were in dire trouble near the bottom of the Premier League table when Sir Alex Ferguson's unbeaten Manchester United arrived for a League Cup quarter-final.

In a performance completely removed from their league form, Avram Grant's Hammers tore into the Red Devils as the snow fell on a freezing night in east London.

Former Manchester United youngster Jonathan Spector started the fun on 22 minutes with a diving header – his first goal for the club – before doubling his tally and West Ham's lead before half-time.

With Nigeria forward Victor Obinna terrorising the visitors, Carlton Cole made it 3-0 eleven minutes after the break before firing in the Hammers' fourth to complete an unforgettable evening of entertainment.

The victory was West Ham's biggest over Manchester United since a 5-1 Division One victory in October 1930.

2014-15 Season Stats

2014/15 season (sub appearances in brackets)

Player	Born	Nat	Former club	BPL Apps	BPL Goals	FAC Apps	FAC Goals	COC Apps	COC Goals
2. Winston Reid	3 July 1988, North Shore, Auckland, New Zealand	NZ	FC Midtjylland (Den)	29 (1)	1	2	-	1	-
3. Aaron Cresswell	15 December 1989, Liverpool, England	Eng	Ipswich Town	38	2	4	-	-	-
4. Kevin Nolan	24 June 1982, Liverpool, England	Eng	Newcastle United	19 (10)	1	3 (1)	-	-	-
5. James Tomkins	29 March 1989, Basildon, England	Eng	Derby County (loan)	20 (2)	1	3	-	-	-
7. Matt Jarvis	22 May 1986, Middlesbrough, England	Eng	Wolverhampton Wanderers	4 (7)	-	-	-	-	-
8. Cheikhou Kouyate	21 December 1989, Dakar, Senegal	Sen	RSC Anderlecht (Bel)	30 (1)	4	1	-	-	-
9. Andy Carroll	6 January 1989, Gateshead, England	Eng	Liverpool	12 (2)	5	2	-	-	-
10. Mauro Zarate	18 March 1987, Haedo, Argentina	Arg	Velez Sarsfield (Arg)	5 (2)	2	-	-	0 (1)	-
11. Stewart Downing	22 July 1984, Middlesbrough, England	Eng	Liverpool	37	6	4	-	0 (1)	-
12. Ricardo Vaz Te	1 October 1986, Lisbon, Portugal	Por	Barnsley	3 (1)	-	-	-	1	-
12. Nene	19 July 1981, Jundiai, Brazil	Bra	Al-Gharafa (Qat)	0 (8)	-	-	-	-	-
13. Adrian	3 January 1987, Seville, Spain	Spa	Real Betis Balompie (Spa)	38	-	4	-	-	-
14. Ravel Morrison	2 February 1993, Wythenshawe, England	Eng	Queens Park Rangers (loan)	0 (1)	-	-	-	1	-
15. Diafra Sakho	24 December 1989, Guediawaye, Senegal	Sen	FC Metz (Fra)	20 (3)	10	1 (1)	1	1	1
16. Mark Noble	8 May 1987, Canning Town, England	Eng	Ipswich Town (loan)	27 (1)	2	4	-	0 (1)	-
17. Joey O'Brien	17 February 1986, Dublin, Republic of Ireland	Ire	Bolton Wanderers	6 (3)	-	0 (2)	-	-	-
18. Carl Jenkinson	8 February 1992, Harlow, England	Eng	Arsenal	29 (3)	-	4	-	-	-
19. James Collins	23 August 1983, Newport, Wales	Wal	Aston Villa	21 (6)	-	2	-	1	-
20. Guy Demel	13 June 1982, Orsay, France	CIv	Hamburger SV (Ger)	3 (3)	-	0 (1)	-	1	-
21. Morgan Amalfitano	20 March 1985, Nice, France	Fra	Olympique Marseille (Fra)	14 (10)	3	1 (3)	-	-	-
21. Mohamed Diame	14 June 1987, Creteil, France	Sen	Wigan Athletic	0 (3)	-	-	-	1	-
22. Jussi Jaaskelainen	19 April 1975, Mikkeli, Finland	Fin	Bolton Wanderers	0 (1)	-	-	-	1	-
23. Diego Poyet	8 April 1995, Zaragoza, Spain	Uru	Charlton Athletic	1 (2)	-	0 (1)	-	1	-
24. Carlton Cole	12 October 1983, Croydon, England	Eng	Chelsea	8 (15)	2	0 (3)	-	1	-
25. Doneil Henry	20 April 1993, Toronto, Ontario, Canada	Can	Apollon Limassol (Cyp)	-	-	-	-	-	-
30. Alex Song	9 September 1987, Douala, Cameron	Cam	Barcelona (Spa)	25 (3)	-	3	-	-	-
31. Enner Valencia	11 January 1989, San Lorenzo, Ecuador	Ecu	Pachuca (Mex)	25 (7)	4	4	-	1	-
32. Reece Burke	2 September 1996, Newham, England	Eng	None	4 (1)	-	-	-	1	-
33. Dan Potts	13 April 1994, Barking, England	Eng	Portsmouth (loan)	-	-	-	-	1	-

2014/15 Premier League Table

Pos	Team	Pld	W	D	L	GF	GA	GD	Pts
1	Chelsea	38	26	9	3	73	32	+41	87
2	Manchester City	38	24	7	7	83	38	+45	79
3	Arsenal	38	22	9	7	71	36	+35	75
4	Manchester United	38	20	10	8	62	37	+25	70
5	Tottenham Hotspur	38	19	7	12	58	53	+5	64
6	Liverpool	38	18	8	12	52	48	+4	62
7	Southampton	38	18	6	14	54	33	+21	60
8	Swansea City	38	16	8	14	46	49	−3	56
9	Stoke City	38	15	9	14	48	45	+3	54
10	Crystal Palace	38	13	9	16	47	51	−4	48
11	Everton	38	12	11	15	48	50	−2	47
12	West Ham United	38	12	11	15	44	47	−3	47
13	West Bromwich Albion	38	11	11	16	38	51	−13	44
14	Leicester City	38	11	8	19	46	55	−9	41
15	Newcastle United	38	10	9	19	40	63	−23	39
16	Sunderland	38	7	17	14	31	53	−22	38
17	Aston Villa	38	10	8	20	31	57	−26	38
18	Hull City	38	8	11	19	33	51	−18	35
19	Burnley	38	7	12	19	28	53	−25	33
20	Queens Park Rangers	38	8	6	24	42	73	−31	30

Spot the Difference Solution

Did you spot the ten differences between the two images of manager Slaven Bilic greeting players inside the West Ham United dressing room?

Where are Hammerhead and Bubbles?